W9-BSS-902

VEGETARIAN COOKING

Photography by Peter Barry
Recipes styled by Helen Burdett
Designed by Richard Hawke
Edited by Jillian Stewart

3258
This 1993 edition produced for Book Express, Inc.
Airport Business Center, 29 Kripes Road, East Granby, Connecticut, USA
Copyright © 1993 CLB Publishing Ltd, Godalming, Surrey, England
All rights reserved
Printed and bound in Hong Kong
USA direct sales rights in this edition are exclusive to Book Express, Inc.
ISBN 1-85833-025-4

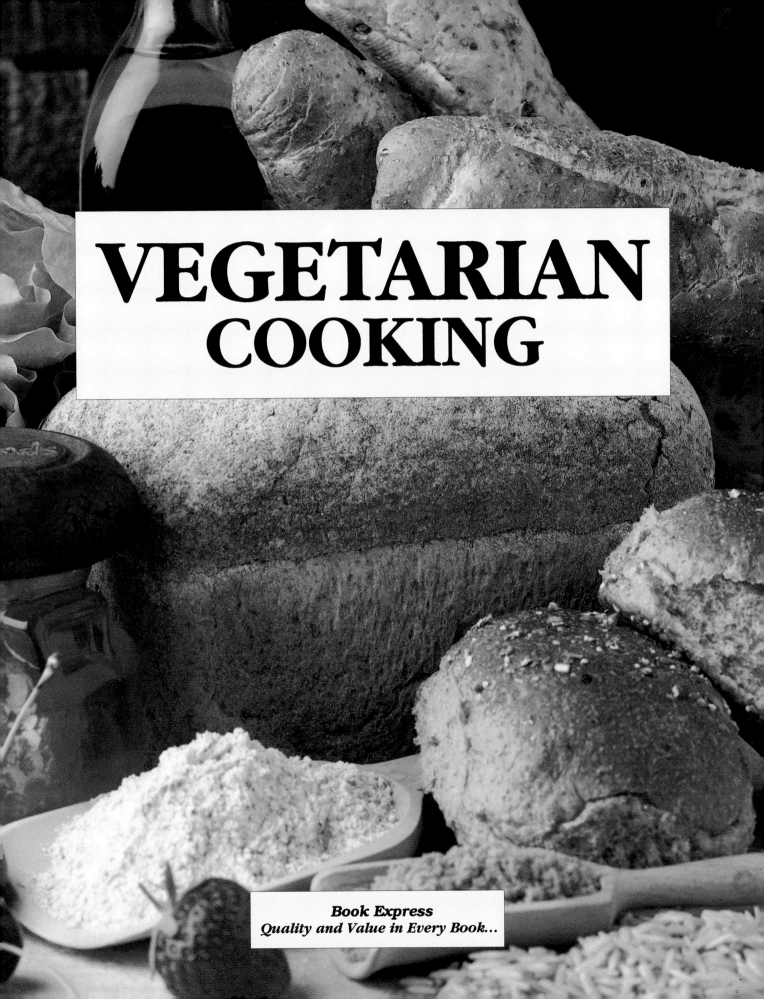

VEGETARIAN COOKING

Book Express
Quality and Value in Every Book...

Contents

Introduction

Vegetarian cooking is growing in popularity as more people realize the health advantages of a meat-free diet. Although people choose to eat vegetarian meals for a variety of reasons – maybe to economize or on moral grounds – the change in diet can be an important move towards a healthier lifestyle.

Contrary to popular opinion, vegetarian food need not be boring or difficult to prepare. Pasta, eggs, cheese, rice, beans, and fruit are as important as vegetables in a vegetarian diet, and they can be utilized to produce healthy, nutritious and interesting meals that will appeal to all ages and tastes.

The mention of vegetarian food makes many people think of rather bland unappetizing food requiring lengthy preparation and careful thought. This need not be so – vegetarian meals can be as simple or as complicated as you wish, and the general guidelines for good nutrition are simple. One of the main reasons a vegetarian diet is considered healthy is because it cuts out cholesterol-rich red meat. However, red meat is a rich source of protein that has to be replaced and not simply left out of your diet.

There are many ways to add protein to a vegetarian diet. Undoubtedly the cheapest and among the most valuable sources of protein are beans and pulses. Not only are they tasty, but they can be used to replace meat in a huge variety of dishes such as chilies, casseroles, and terrines. Cheese and eggs can be incorporated into appetizers and desserts as well as main courses, although care must be taken not to eat too many eggs or too much rich, fatty cheese. One of the most useful advances in meat-free protein is the growth in popularity of products such as tofu, which is healthy, low in fat and, because it absorbs flavors well, can be adapted to a whole variety of dishes.

You will find a wealth of ideas within these pages to add interest to your weekly menus. So whether it is a quick snack or a family meal, these imaginative easy-to-follow recipes ensure that producing the perfect vegetarian dish is simplicity itself.

CREAM OF CARROT SOUP

A classic soup which is suitable for any occasion.

SERVES 4

---

1 large onion, chopped
2 cloves garlic, crushed
1 tbsp olive oil
2½ cups carrots, chopped
½ tsp dried mixed herbs
3¾ cups vegetable stock
⅔ cup sour cream
Salt and pepper

1. Heat the oil in a large, heavy-bottomed pan and sauté the chopped onion and garlic until transparent.

2. Add the carrots, mixed herbs and stock.

3. Bring to a boil and simmer, covered, for about 30 minutes until the carrots are soft.

4. Cool a little and then purée in a blender or food processor until smooth.

5. Add the sour cream, season to taste and mix thoroughly.

6. Heat through gently and serve.

TIME: Preparation takes about 10 minutes, cooking takes 35 minutes.

WATCHPOINT: Do not allow the soup to boil after adding the sour cream.

VARIATION: For a richer soup, omit the sour cream and add a swirl of heavy cream just before serving.

WILD RICE SOUP

A meal in itself when served with whole-grain bread and a green salad.

SERVES 4

¼ cup wild rice
2 cups water
2 onions, chopped
1 tbsp butter or margarine
2 celery stalks, chopped
½ tsp dried thyme
½ tsp dried sage
3¾ cups water or vegetable stock
1 vegetable bouillon cube
1 tbsp shoyu sauce (Japanese soy sauce)
6 small potatoes, peeled and coarsely
  chopped
1 carrot, finely diced
Milk or light cream

1. Add the wild rice to the 2 cups of water, bring to a boil, reduce the heat and simmer for 40-50 minutes until the rice has puffed and most of the liquid has been absorbed.

2. Heat the butter in a large, heavy-bottomed pot and sauté the onions until transparent.

3. Add the celery, thyme and sage, and cook for 5-10 minutes, stirring often.

4. Add the water, bouillon cube, shoyu sauce and potatoes.

5. Bring to a boil and simmer for 20 minutes or until the potatoes are cooked.

6. Purée the mixture in a food processor or blender until smooth.

7. Return to the pot, add the carrot and wild rice.

8. Add the milk or cream to thin the soup to the desired consistency.

9. Reheat gently and serve.

TIME: Preparation takes about 15 minutes, cooking takes 30 minutes plus 40 minutes to cook the wild rice.

COOK'S TIP: You can prepare and cook the soup while the wild rice is cooking. Add the rice to the soup at the end of the cooking time.

FREEZING: Cook a large quantity of wild rice and freeze in small portions. Add to the soup or other dishes as needed.

VARIATION: Toast some sliced almonds and sprinkle on top of the soup before serving.

FRENCH ONION SOUP

*This soup tastes best if cooked the day
before it is needed and then reheated as required.*

SERVES 4

---

3 medium onions
4 tbsps butter or margarine
2 tbsps all-purpose flour or soya flour
4⅓ cups boiling vegetable stock or
   water plus 2 bouillon cubes
Salt and pepper

Topping
4 slices French bread, cut crosswise
½ cup cheddar cheese, grated
¼ cup Parmesan cheese, grated

---

1. Slice the onions very finely into rings.

2. Melt the butter in a heavy-bottomed pot, add the onion rings and fry over a medium heat until well browned.

3. Mix in the flour and stir well until browned.

4. Add the stock and seasoning, bring to a boil and simmer for 30 minutes.

5. Toast the bread on both sides.

6. Combine the cheeses, and spread over the bread slices; broil until golden brown.

7. Place the slices of bread and cheese in the bottom of individual soup dishes and spoon the soup over the top.

8. Serve at once.

TIME: Preparation takes 10 minutes, cooking takes 30 minutes.

VARIATION: For a special occasion, add a tablespoonful of brandy to the stock.

WATCHPOINT: The onions must be very well browned, as this
gives the rich color to the soup.

CAULIFLOWER AND BROCCOLI SOUFFLETTES

Serve as a wintertime first course or as a main meal with rice salad and ratatouille.

SERVES 6

12 oz cauliflower
12 oz broccoli
4 tbsps margarine
½ cup whole-wheat or brown rice flour
Scant 2 cups milk
½ cup cheddar cheese, grated
1 large egg, separated
Good pinch of nutmeg
Salt and pepper

1. Break the cauliflower and broccoli into small florets and steam until just tender – about 7-10 minutes.

2. Melt the margarine in a saucepan, remove from the heat and gradually add the flour. Stir to a roux and add the milk gradually, blending well to ensure a smooth consistency.

3. Return the saucepan to the heat and stir until the sauce thickens and comes to a boil.

4. Cool a little and add the egg yolk and cheese, stir well and add nutmeg to taste.

5. Whip the egg white until stiff and fold carefully into the sauce.

6. Place the vegetables into 6 small buttered ramekin dishes and season.

7. Divide the sauce evenly among the dishes and bake immediately at 375°F for about 35 minutes until puffed and golden.

8. Serve at once.

TIME: Preparation takes 15 minutes, cooking takes 50 minutes.

DATE, APPLE AND CELERY APPETIZER

A healthy dish with a tasty mix of flavors.

SERVES 4

4 tsps finely grated coconut
2 crisp eating apples
3-4 celery stalks
¾ cup dates
2 tbsps plain yogurt
Salt and pepper
Pinch of nutmeg

1. Toast the coconut in a dry frying pan over a low heat until it is golden brown, then put to one side.

2. Core and dice the apples and chop the celery finely.

3. Plunge the dates into boiling water, drain and chop finely.

4. Combine the apples, celery and dates in a mixing bowl.

5. Add the yogurt, seasoning and nutmeg and mix thoroughly so that the salad is coated completely.

6. Transfer to a serving bowl and garnish with the toasted coconut.

7. Serve at once.

TIME: Preparation takes 10 minutes, cooking takes 2-3 minutes.

SERVING IDEA: Serve individual portions on a bed of watercress.

COOK'S TIP: Red skinned apples add color to this salad.

INDONESIAN-STYLE STUFFED PEPPERS

For this adaptable recipe you can substitute
pine nuts or peanuts if you don't have cashews.

SERVES 8 AS AN APPETIZER

2 tbsps olive oil
1 medium onion, peeled and chopped
1 clove garlic, crushed
2 tsps turmeric
1 tsp crushed coriander seeds
4 tbsps flaked coconut
1½ cups mushrooms, chopped
¾ cup bulgar wheat
½ cup raisins
1¼ cups vegetable stock or water
2-3 tomatoes, skinned and chopped
½ cup cashew nuts
4 small green peppers, de-seeded and cut
   in half lenthwise
2 tsps lemon juice
Vegetable stock for cooking

1. Heat the oil in a saucepan and fry the onion and garlic until lightly browned.

2. Add the turmeric, coriander and coconut, and cook gently for about 2 minutes.

3. Add the mushrooms and bulgar wheat and cook for a further 2 minutes.

4. Add the raisins, stock or water, and tomatoes and simmer gently for 15-20 minutes until the bulgar wheat is cooked.

5. Toast the cashew nuts in a dry frying pan over a low heat until golden brown.

6. Blanch the peppers in boiling water for 3 minutes.

7. Mix the nuts and lemon juice with the rest of the ingredients and fill the peppers with the mixture.

8. Place the filled peppers on the bottom of a large casserole dish and pour stock around the peppers.

9. Bake at 350°F for 20 minutes.

10. Drain peppers and place on a hot plate to serve.

TIME: Preparation takes 20 minutes, cooking takes 45 minutes.

FREEZING: The cooked peppers will freeze well for up to 3 months.

WATERCRESS AND MUSHROOM PÂTÉ

*A delightful pâté which is perfect garnished with lime
or lemon wedges and served with thinly
sliced whole-wheat bread and butter.*

SERVES 4

4 tbsps butter
1 medium onion, finely chopped
2½ cups large mushrooms, finely chopped
1 bunch watercress, finely chopped
1 cup low fat cream cheese
Few drops shoyu sauce (Japanese soy
   sauce)
Scant ½ tsp caraway seeds
Black pepper

1. Melt the butter in a saucepan over a low heat and cook the onion until soft but not colored.

2. Raise the heat, add the mushrooms and cook quickly for 2 minutes.

3. Put in the chopped watercress and stir for about 30 seconds until it becomes limp.

4. Place the contents of the saucepan in a blender or food processor together with the cheese and shoyu sauce.

5. Purée until smooth.

6. Stir in the caraway seeds and pepper to taste.

7. Put into individual ramekin dishes or one large serving dish and chill for at least 2 hours until firm.

TIME: Preparation takes 10 minutes, cooking takes 5 minutes.

COOK'S TIP: It may be necessary to scrape down the ingredients several times while processing as the mixture will be fairly thick.

BRAZILIAN AVOCADOS

The perfect way to impress your dinner guests
right from the first course.

SERVES 4

2 large ripe avocados
A little lemon juice
Salt and pepper
½ cup finely chopped Brazil nuts
½ cup cheddar cheese, grated
2 tbsps Parmesan cheese
2 tbsps freshly chopped parsley
2 firm ripe tomatoes, skinned and finely
   chopped
Whole-wheat breadcrumbs
2 tbsps melted butter
A little paprika

1. Halve the avocados and carefully remove the flesh from the skins. Brush the inside of the skins with a little of the lemon juice.

2. Dice the avocado and put into a bowl with a sprinkling of lemon juice and the seasoning.

3. Add the nuts, cheeses, parsley and tomatoes.

4. Mix gently.

5. Spoon the filling into the avocado shells, sprinkle with the breadcrumbs and drizzle the butter over the top.

6. Dust with the paprika and bake at 400°F for 15 minutes.

TIME: Preparation takes about 10 minutes, cooking takes 15 minutes.

COOK'S TIP: Do not prepare this dish too far in advance as the avocado may discolor.

SERVING IDEA: Serve with a little salad as an appetizer or with a rice pilaff,
vegetables and tossed salad for a main course.

SAVORY TOMATOES

An ideal appetizer for dieters.

SERVES 4

4 large beefsteak tomatoes
4 tbsps cottage cheese
1 tsp ground cumin
1 green pepper, de-seeded and diced
Salt and pepper
¼ cup pumpkin seeds
1 bunch watercress
Milk

1. Slice off the tops of the tomatoes.

2. Remove the seeds and leave upside down to drain.

3. Rub the cottage cheese through a strainer to achieve a smooth consistency, adding a little milk if necessary.

4. Stir in the cumin, pepper and seasoning.

5. Divide the mixture into four and stuff the tomatoes.

6. Dry roast the pumpkin seeds in a frying pan over low heat until they are lightly browned. Sprinkle over the tomatoes.

7. Chill until required.

8. Serve on a bed of watercress.

TIME: Preparation takes 10 minutes.

SERVING IDEA: Serve with very thin slices of whole-wheat bread and butter.

VARIATION: Use cream cheese in place of the cottage cheese.

MUSHROOMS AND TOFU IN GARLIC BUTTER

A quick and delicious first course.

SERVES 4

3 cups small mushrooms
1 inch piece fresh ginger
8 oz tofu (bean curd)
1 stick butter
4 small cloves garlic, crushed
2 tbsps fresh parsley, chopped

1. Wipe the mushrooms with a damp cloth.

2. Peel and grate the ginger.

3. Cut the smoked tofu into small ½-inch squares.

4. Melt the butter in a frying pan.

5. Add the garlic and ginger and fry gently for two minutes.

6. Add the mushrooms and cook gently for 4-5 minutes until the mushrooms are softened.

7. Finally, add the smoked tofu and heat through.

8. Divide among 4 individually heated dishes, sprinkle with chopped parsley and serve at once.

TIME: Preparation takes 10 minutes, cooking takes 12 minutes.

SERVING IDEA: Serve with French bread or crusty whole-wheat rolls.

VARIATION: Substitute asparagus tips for the mushrooms.

SPICY BLACK-EYED PEAS

A spicy dish from the West Indies – perfect as a snack.

SERVES 4

2 cups black-eyed peas, soaked and cooked
4 tbsps vegetable oil
1 large onion, finely chopped
2 cloves garlic, crushed
1 tsp ground cinnamon
½ tsp ground cumin
Salt and pepper
⅔ cup bean liquid or water
2 tbsps tomato paste
1 tbsp shoyu sauce (Japanese soy sauce)
2 large tomatoes, skinned and chopped
1 tbsp fresh parsley, chopped

1. Drain the beans well and retain the cooking liquid.

2. Heat the oil in a heavy-bottomed pan and fry the onion and garlic for 4-5 minutes until soft.

3. Stir in the cinnamon, cumin and seasoning and cook for a further 2 minutes.

4. Add the beans, bean stock, tomato paste, shoyu sauce and tomatoes.

5. Stir and bring to a boil.

6. Simmer for 15-20 minutes until thick.

7. Check the seasoning and adjust to taste.

8. Serve sprinkled with chopped parsley.

TIME: Preparation takes 20 minutes, cooking time, including the beans, 1 hour 35 minutes.

SERVING IDEA: Serve over pasta or rice.

VARIATION: Navy beans can be used in place of black-eyed peas.

MIXED NUT BALLS

*This versatile dish can be made in advance and
refrigerated until required for cooking.*
SERVES 8

⅔ cup ground almonds
⅔ cup ground hazelnuts
⅔ cup ground pecans
¾ cup whole-wheat breadcrumbs
1 cup cheddar cheese, grated
1 egg, beaten
4-5 tbsps dry sherry or 2 tbsps milk and 3
    tbsps dry sherry
1 small onion, finely chopped
1 tbsp fresh ginger, grated
1 tbsp fresh parsley, chopped
1 small red or green chili pepper,
    finely chopped
1 medium red pepper, diced
1 tsp sea salt
1 tsp freshly ground black pepper

1. Mix the almonds, hazelnuts and pecans
together with the breadcrumbs and the
cheese.

2. In another bowl, mix the beaten egg
with the sherry, onion, ginger, parsley,
chili and red pepper.

3. Combine with the nut mixture and add
the salt and pepper.

4. If the mixture is too dry, add a little
more sherry or milk.

5. Form into small 1-inch balls.

6. Do not preheat the oven.

7. Arrange the balls on a well-greased
baking sheet and bake at 350°F for about
20-25 minutes, until golden brown.

TIME: Preparation takes about 20 minutes, cooking takes 20-25 minutes.

SERVING IDEA: Serve on individual plates on a bed of chopped lettuce. Garnish with slices
of lemon and pass around your favorite sauce in a separate bowl.

PEANUT RISOTTO

A crunchy textured dish to serve on the side.

SERVES 4

1 large onion, chopped
1 clove garlic, crushed
1 tbsp vegetable oil
¾ cup short grain brown rice
1 cup peanuts, roughly chopped
1½ cups mushrooms, sliced
2½ cups boiling water
¾ cup green beans
¼ cup raisins
2 tsps dried oregano
2 tsps lemon juice
Salt and pepper

1. Heat the oil in a heavy-bottomed pot and fry the onion and garlic for 3-4 minutes.

2. Add the rice and peanuts to brown for 1-2 minutes.

3. Add the mushrooms and cook for a further 3-4 minutes, then add the boiling water, stir once and simmer for 30 minutes.

4. Add the beans, raisins, herbs, lemon juice and seasoning and cook for a further 5-10 minutes.

TIME: Preparation takes 10 minutes, cooking takes 50 minutes.

SERVING IDEA: Serve garnished with lemon wedges and parsley.

VARIATION: Use this mixture to stuff cabbage, spinach or vine leaves.

DHINGRI KARI (MUSHROOM CURRY)

An ideal snack or supper dish.

SERVES 4

1½ cups leeks, finely sliced
2 cloves garlic, crushed
½ tsp fresh ginger, grated
2 tsps curry powder
1 tsp garam masala
2 tbsps oil
6 cups mushrooms, cut into quarters
½ cup coconut, grated
1 cup water
1 tbsp lemon juice

---

1. Heat the oil in a saucepan and fry the leeks, garlic, ginger and spices until soft.

2. Add the mushrooms and cook over a low heat until soft.

3. Add the grated coconut and half of the water. Cook gently until the coconut has completely softened, adding extra water if the mixture appears too dry.

4. Stir in the lemon juice and sufficient salt to taste.

5. Serve on a bed of rice.

TIME: Preparation takes 15 minutes, cooking takes about 20 minutes.

SERVING IDEA: Serve with a tomato and onion salad.

PARSNIP FRITTERS

These tasty fritters make a nice change for lunch or a light snack.

SERVES 4

---

1 cup all-purpose flour
2 tsps baking powder
1 tsp salt
½ tsp pepper
1 egg
⅔ cup milk
1 tbsp melted butter
3-4 cooked parsnips, finely diced
Oil or clarified butter for frying

---

1. Mix together the flour, baking powder, salt and pepper.

2. Beat the egg and mix with the milk and melted butter.

3. Stir this mixture into the dry ingredients.

4. Stir in the cooked parsnips.

5. Divide the mixture into 16 and shape into small fritters.

6. Fry in oil or clarified butter until browned on both sides.

TIME: Preparation takes 10 minutes, cooking takes about 5-8 minutes per batch.

VARIATION: Zucchini, corn, onions or eggplant may be substituted for the parsnips.

SERVING IDEA: Serve with yogurt sauce or make them slightly larger and serve as a main course with salad.

BULGAR RISOTTO

*This makes a quick lunch dish and is
particularly handy if unexpected guests call.*

SERVES 3-4

1 cup bulgar wheat
Boiling water
1 medium onion, peeled and finely
   chopped
2 celery stalks, finely chopped
1-2 cloves garlic, crushed
1 tbsp butter
1 small red pepper, diced
1 small green pepper, diced
½ tsp dried mixed herbs
½ cup peanuts, chopped
1 vegetable bouillon cube dissolved in
   ¼ cup boiling water
2 tsps shoyu sauce (Japanese soy sauce)
½ cup corn
½ cup peas
Salt and pepper
Juice of half a lemon

1. Put the bulgar wheat into a bowl and
cover with boiling water.

2. Leave for about 10 minutes until the
water is absorbed and the wheat swollen.

3. Meanwhile, heat the butter in a
saucepan and sauté the onion, celery and
garlic for a few minutes.

4. Add the peppers, herbs, nuts and
vegetable stock.

5. Simmer over a low heat for about 8
minutes.

6. Add the bulgar wheat, shoyu, corn,
peas and seasoning and mix together well.

7. Continue cooking for another 5
minutes.

8. Mix in the lemon juice and transfer to a
heated serving dish.

9. Serve immediately.

TIME: Preparation takes 15 minutes, cooking takes 20 minutes.

SERVING IDEA: Serve with a crisp green salad.

WATCHPOINT: If the risotto is too dry, add a little more water or stock.

LIMA BEAN FIESTA

*Serve this dish on its own as an appetizer or as
a snack with lots of crusty bread.*

SERVES 4

1 cup young lima beans, soaked overnight
1 medium onion
1 clove garlic
Half a cucumber
2 tbsps fresh parsley, chopped or 1 tsp dried
2 tbsps fresh mint, chopped
2 tbsps olive oil
Juice and grated rind of l lemon
Salt
Freshly ground black pepper
Watercress to garnish

1. Cook the beans in plenty of boiling water for about 1 hour or until just tender.

2. Drain and put into a mixing bowl.

3. Peel and finely chop the onion.

4. Crush the garlic and chop the cucumber into bite-sized pieces.

5. Add the onion, garlic, cucumber, herbs, oil, lemon juice and rind to the beans and mix well.

6. Add seasoning to taste and leave to marinate in the refrigerator for 2 hours.

7. Transfer to a clean serving bowl.

8. Serve garnished with watercress.

TIME: Preparation takes 15 minutes, marinating takes 2 hours and cooking takes 1 hour.

VARIATION: Substitute red kidney beans or black-eyed peas for the lima beans.

Pasta and Avocado Salad

The perfect lunch or supper salad for guests.

SERVES 4

2 cups pasta shapes
3 tbsps mayonnaise
2 tsps tahini (sesame paste)
1 orange
½ medium red pepper
1 medium avocado
Pumpkin seeds to garnish

1. Cook the pasta until tender and leave to cool.

2. Mix together the mayonnaise and tahini.

3. Chop the orange into small pieces, retaining any juice.

4. Chop the pepper.

5. Stir the mayonnaise mixture, pepper and orange (plus juice) into the pasta.

6. Just before serving, cube the avocado and stir in carefully.

7. Serve on an oval platter, decorated with pumpkin seeds.

TIME: Preparation takes 10 minutes, cooking takes about 35 minutes.

WATCHPOINT: Do not peel the avocado until required as it may discolor.

VARIATION: Green pepper may be used in place of the red pepper.

TABOULEH

This is a traditional salad from the Middle East. The main ingredient is bulgar which is partially cooked cracked wheat and only needs soaking for a short while before it is ready to eat.

SERVES 6

¾ cup bulgar wheat
1 tsp salt
1½ cups boiling water
1 lb tomatoes, chopped
1 cucumber, diced
3-4 green onions, chopped

Dressing
¼ cup olive oil
¼ cup lemon juice
2 tbsps fresh mint
4 tbsps fresh parsley
2 cloves garlic, crushed

1. Mix the bulgar wheat with the salt, pour over the boiling water and leave for 15-20 minutes. All the water will then be absorbed.

2. Mix together the ingredients for the dressing and pour over the soaked bulgar.

3. Fold in lightly with a spoon.

4. Leave for two hours or overnight in a fridge or cool place.

5. Mix in the tomatoes, cucumber and green onions and serve.

TIME: Preparation takes about 20 minutes, standing time is about 2 hours.

COOK'S TIP: A few cooked beans can be added to make this dish more substantial.

SERVING IDEA: Serve with pizzas, quiches and roasts.

BAVARIAN POTATO SALAD

It is best to prepare this salad a few hours in advance to allow the potatoes to absorb the flavors.

SERVES 4-6

2 lbs small new potatoes
4 tbsps olive oil
4 green onions, finely chopped
1 clove garlic, crushed
2 tbsps fresh dill, chopped or 1 tbsp dried
2 tbsps white wine vinegar
½ tsp sugar
Salt and pepper
2 tbsps fresh parsley, chopped

1. Wash the potatoes but do not peel, put them into a pan, cover with water and boil until just tender.

2. While the potatoes are cooking, heat the olive oil in a frying pan and cook the green onions and garlic for 2-3 minutes until they have softened a little.

3. Add the dill and cook gently for a further minute.

4. Add the wine vinegar and sugar, and stir until the sugar dissolves. Remove from the heat and add a little seasoning.

5. Drain the potatoes and pour the dressing over them while they are still hot.

6. Allow to cool and sprinkle with the chopped parsley before serving.

TIME: Preparation takes 15 minutes, cooking takes 15 minutes.

WHEATBERRY SALAD

This makes a substantial salad dish which provides an almost perfect protein balance.

SERVES 4

1 cup wheatberries, cooked
½ cup kidney beans, cooked
3 medium tomatoes
4 green onions, chopped
2 celery stalks, chopped
1 tbsp pumpkin seeds

Dressing
4 tbsps olive or sunflower oil
2 tbsps red wine vinegar
1 clove garlic, crushed
1 tsp fresh ginger, grated
1 tsp paprika
1 tbsp shoyu sauce (Japanese soy sauce)
Fresh or dried oregano, to taste
Freshly ground black pepper

1. Mix the salad ingredients together, reserving a few pumpkin seeds and green onions for garnishing.

2. Mix the dressing ingredients vigorously.

3. Pour over the salad and mix gently.

TIME: Preparation takes 20 minutes.

SERVING IDEA: Serve with a lettuce salad.
Wheatberries also mix well with grated carrot and an orange dressing.

COOK'S TIP: This salad keeps well so it can be made in advance and kept in the refrigerator until required.

BUYING GUIDE: Wheatberries are available in health food stores.
If you cannot obtain them use millet.

SPINACH SALAD

Serve with a simple main course.

SERVES 4-6

1 lb spinach
1 medium red cabbage
1 medium onion
1 cup fresh apricots
4 tbsps olive oil mixed with 1½ tbsps
    white wine vinegar
½ cup toasted sunflower seeds

1. Wash the spinach and drain well.

2. First remove the outer leaves and core, then slice the cabbage finely.

3. Slice the onion finely and cut the apricots into slivers.

4. Tear the spinach leaves into bite-sized pieces and put into a serving dish.

5. Add the sliced cabbage, onion and apricots.

6. Pour over the oil and vinegar dressing and mix together thoroughly.

7. Sprinkle with sunflower seeds and serve.

TIME: Preparation takes 15 minutes.

WATCHPOINT: Spinach leaves bruise easily so take care when washing and tearing the leaves.

TOFU SALAD

A tasty main course salad. Serve with whole-grain bread.

SERVES 4-6

2 cups broccoli florets
1½ cups mushrooms
4 oz can pineapple rings
4 tbsps canned corn
3 tbsps olive oil mixed with 1 tbsp white
  wine vinegar
1 large packet tofu, cut into cubes

1. Cover the broccoli florets with boiling water and leave to stand for 5 minutes. Drain and allow to cool.

2. Wipe the mushrooms with a clean cloth and slice thinly.

3. Drain the pineapple and cut into small pieces.

4. Put the broccoli, mushrooms, pineapple and corn into a large bowl together with the dressing.

5. Mix carefully.

6. Divide the salad among 4 individual dishes and place the smoked tofu on top.

7. Serve at once.

TIME: Preparation takes 15 minutes.

VARIATION: Omit the tofu and serve as a side salad with quiches.

Crunchy Cabbage Salad

Serve this very attractive salad for a party or as part of a buffet.

SERVES 4-6

---

1 large red cabbage
1 green pepper, de-seeded and chopped
½ small pineapple, peeled and finely chopped
Segments from 2 medium oranges
6 green onions, finely chopped
3 celery stalks, chopped
½ cup hazelnuts, coarsely chopped
½ cup sprouted aduki beans

Dressing
½ cup mayonnaise
¼ cup thick plain yogurt
Salt and pepper

---

1. Remove any tough or discolored outer leaves from the cabbage.

2. Trim the base so that the cabbage will stand upright, and cut about a quarter off the top.

3. Using a sharp knife, scoop out the inside of the cabbage leaving ¼ inch for the shell. Set the shell aside.

4. Discard any tough pieces and shred the remaining cabbage very finely.

5. Put the shredded cabbage into a large bowl together with the pepper, pineapple, orange segments, green onions, celery, hazelnuts and beans.

6. Mix the mayonnaise, yogurt and seasoning together and carefully fold into the vegetables and fruit.

7. Put the mixture into the cabbage shell and place on a serving dish garnished with parsley.

TIME: Preparation takes 20 minutes.

WATCHPOINT: If preparing in advance, refrigerate the salad and dressing separately and mix them together just before serving.

VARIATION: Walnuts may be used in place of hazelnuts but add them when mixing the salad and dressing together.

SPROUTED LENTIL SALAD

A quick and easy salad.

SERVES 4-6

2 cups broccoli florets
1 red pepper
1 cup sprouted lentils
½ cup golden raisins
3 tbsps olive oil mixed with 1 tbsp white
    wine vinegar
1 tsp freshly grated ginger

1. Cover the broccoli florets with boiling water and leave to stand for 5 minutes. Drain and cool.

2. Core and de-seed the pepper and dice.

3. Arrange the sprouted lentils on a serving dish.

4. Mix together the broccoli, pepper and raisins and pile in the center.

5. Mix the grated ginger with the dressing and pour over the salad.

6. Serve at once.

TIME: Preparation takes 15 minutes.

SERVING IDEA: Serve with pastry based dishes.

VARIATION: Cauliflower florets may be used instead of broccoli.

SESAME SPROUT SALAD

Serve as an accompaniment to a hot main dish.

SERVES 4-6

2 medium carrots, peeled
1 green pepper
½ cup dried apricots
1 tbsp sesame seeds
2 cups beansprouts
3 tbsps olive oil mixed with 1 tbsp white
    wine vinegar
2 tbsps pineapple juice

1. Cut the carrots into julienne.

2. De-seed and slice the pepper thinly.

3. Cut the apricots into slivers.

4. Toast the sesame seeds in a dry pan over a low heat until they are golden brown and give off a delicious aroma.

5. Place the carrots, pepper, apricots and beansprouts in a serving dish.

6. Mix the dressing with the pinapple juice and fold into the salad.

7. Sprinkle the sesame seeds over the top.

8. Serve at once.

TIME: Preparation takes 10 minutes.

COOK'S TIP: Use beansprouts which are at least 1 inch long for this recipe.

INDIAN VEGETABLE CURRY

A wonderfully tasty curry which has the added
advantage of freezing well.

SERVES 4

Spices
2 tsps turmeric
1 tsp cumin
1 tsp mustard seed
1 tsp fenugreek
4 tsps coriander
½ tsp chili powder
1 tsp ginger
1 tsp black peppercorns

1 lb onions, finely chopped
Vegetable oil (vary amount to suit
　– about 4 tbsps)
1¼ cups evaporated milk
2 tbsps white wine vinegar
14 oz can crushed tomatoes
1 tbsp tomato paste
2 tsps brown sugar
1 vegetable bouillon cube dissolved
　in little boiling water
4 cups chopped mushrooms or mixed
　vegetables (e.g. mushrooms,
　cauliflower, carrots, potatoes, okra)

1. Grind all the spices together. This amount will make 3 tbsps of curry powder.

2. Heat the oil in a heavy-bottomed pot and fry the onions until golden.

3. Add the ground spices, lower the heat and cook for 3 minutes, stirring all the time.

4. Add the milk and vinegar and stir well.

5. Add the tomatoes, tomato paste, sugar and stock.

6. Bring to the boil, cover and simmer very gently for 1 hour.

7. Add the vegetables and cook until tender – about 30 minutes.

TIME: Preparation takes 30 minutes, cooking takes 1 hour 30 minutes.

SERVING IDEA: Serve with boiled brown rice, chappatis or poppadoms and Cucumber Raita. Cucumber Raita – combine diced cucumber with yogurt, a little chopped mint, a pinch of chili powder, cumin and seasoning to taste.

FREEZING: The curry sauce will freeze well for up to 3 months so it is worth making double the quantity.

CORN AND PARSNIP QUICHE

Serve this unusual quiche with jacket potatoes
filled with cottage cheese and chives.

SERVES 6

Pie Crust
⅓ cup soft margarine
1½ cups whole-wheat flour
1 tsp baking powder
Pinch of salt
4-6 tbsps ice-cold water
1 tbsp oil

Filling
1 large onion, peeled and finely chopped
1 clove garlic, crushed
2 tbsps butter or margarine
2 large parsnips, steamed and mashed
1 cup corn, frozen or canned
1 tsp dried basil
Salt and pepper
3 eggs
⅔ cup milk
¾ cup grated cheddar cheese
1 medium tomato, sliced

1. Rub the margarine into the flour, baking powder and salt until the mixture resembles fine breadcrumbs.

2. Add the water and oil and work together lightly. The mixture should be fairly moist.

3. Leave for half an hour.

4. Roll out and line a 10 inch pie plate.

5. Prick the bottom and bake at 425°F for about 8 minutes.

6. Meanwhile, heat the butter or margarine in a saucepan and sauté the onion and garlic until soft and golden.

7. Add the parsnips, corn and basil, season to taste and heat gently.

8. Beat the eggs and add the milk.

9. Add to the vegetable mixture and stir over a low heat until the mixture just begins to set.

10. Pour into the crust and top with the grated cheese and sliced tomato.

11. Bake at 375°F for 15-20 minutes or until the cheese is golden brown.

TIME: Preparation takes about 40 minutes, cooking takes 30 minutes.

COOK'S TIP: The partial cooking of the whole mixture helps to keep the crust from becoming soggy and considerably reduces the cooking time.

Sweet Potato and Green Bean Turnovers

These savory pies are a tasty addition to any lunch box or picnic basket.

SERVES 4

Whole-wheat dough for a 10 inch single crust pie (see recipe for Corn and Parsnip Quiche)
½ medium onion, finely chopped
1 clove garlic, crushed
1 tbsp oil
½ tsp freshly grated ginger
¼ – ½ tsp chili powder
¼ tsp turmeric
½ tsp ground cumin
1 tsp ground coriander
¼ tsp dry mustard
1 medium-sized sweet potato, cooked and finely diced
½ cup green beans, chopped into ½ inch lengths
2 tbsps vegetable stock or water
Salt and pepper

1. Heat the oil in a saucepan and fry the onion and garlic until soft.

2. Add the ginger and all the spices and stir.

3. Add the diced potato, beans and water or stock and cook gently for 4-5 minutes or until the beans begin to cook.

4. Allow the mixture to cool and season well.

5. Roll out the dough into 4 circles.

6. Place a quarter of the filling in the center of each circle and dampen the edges of the dough with a little water.

7. Join the dough together over the filling.

8. Make a small hole in each pie and glaze with milk or egg.

9. Bake for 15-20 minutes at 400°F.

TIME: Preparation, including making the dough, takes 25 minutes.
Cooking takes 15-20 minutes.

FREEZING: The pies will freeze well for up to 2 months. Thaw at room temperature.

CARROT AND CASHEW NUT ROAST

*A delicious roast to serve hot, but the full flavor of
the caraway seeds and lemon are more prominent
when the roast is served cold.*

SERVES 6

1 medium-sized onion, chopped
1-2 cloves garlic, crushed
1 tbsp olive or sunflower oil
2 cups carrots, cooked and mashed
2 cups cashew nuts, ground
1 cup whole-wheat breadcrumbs
1 tbsp light tahini (sesame paste)
1½ tsps caraway seeds
1 tsp yeast extract
Juice of ½ a lemon
⅓ cup stock from the carrots or water
Salt and pepper

1. Heat oil in a frying pan and fry the
onion and garlic until soft.

2. Mix together with all the other
ingredients and season to taste.

3. Place the mixture in a greased 2 lb loaf
pan.

4. Cover with foil and bake at 350°F for 1
hour.

5. Remove the foil and bake for a further
10 minutes.

6. Leave to stand in the loaf pan for at
least 10 minutes before turning out.

TIME: Preparation takes 20 minutes, cooking takes 1 hour 10 minutes.

FREEZING: This loaf can be frozen at the end of Step 3. When required, remove
from the freezer and thaw overnight in the refrigerator then continue from
Step 4. It can also be frozen at the end of Step 6.

SERVING IDEA: Serve hot with roast potatoes and a green vegetable, or
cold with a mixed green salad.

PERFECT POTATOES

*Potatoes become extra special when teamed
up with the flavor of onion.*

SERVES 5

6 medium potatoes
1 large onion
Salt and pepper
1¼ cups milk
1½ tbsps butter or margarine

1. Peel and finely slice the potatoes and onion.

2. Layer the potato slices and onion in a shallow ovenproof dish, sprinkling each layer with some salt and pepper.

3. Pour over the milk and dot with the butter or margarine.

4. Bake uncovered in a preheated oven, 350°F for 1-1½ hours or until the potatoes are soft, golden and brown on top.

TIME: Preparation takes 15 minutes, cooking takes 1-1½ hours.

SERVING IDEA: Serve with broiled mushrooms and tomatoes for a supper dish or serve with roasts, burgers or pies.

FREEZING: Cook quickly, cover with foil and place in a freezer bag. Thaw at room temperature for 4-6 hours and reheat at 375°F for about 30 minutes.

VARIATION: Place a layer of finely sliced cooking apples in the bottom of the dish.

DEEP MUSHROOM PIE

A delicious pie and so adaptable. Serve with
salad or potatoes and a green vegetable.

SERVES 4

Filling
1 tbsp vegetable oil
4½ cups mushrooms, cleaned and
    chopped
2 cups mixed nuts, ground
2 medium onions, peeled and finely
    chopped
1 cup whole-wheat breadcrumbs
2 eggs, beaten
1 tsp dried thyme or 2 tsps fresh
1 tsp dried marjoram or 2 tsps fresh
1 tbsp shoyu sauce (Japanese soy sauce)
Salt and pepper to taste
Small quantity of vegetable stock to
    achieve right consistency if necessary

Crust
3 cups whole-wheat flour
Pinch of salt
1 tsp baking powder (optional)
½ cup solid vegetable shortening
½ cup water plus extra boiling water
    as necessary
Beaten egg to glaze

1. Heat the oil in a large saucepan and gently fry the onion until soft.

2. Add the finely chopped mushrooms and cook until the juices begin to run.

3. Remove from the heat and add all the other filling ingredients to form a thick, but not dry, consistency, adding a little stock or water if necessary. Allow to cool.

4. To prepare the dough, first sift the flour, salt and baking powder into a large mixing bowl.

5. Cut the shortening into small pieces and melt in a saucepan. Add the cold water and bring to a fierce, rolling boil.

6. Immediately pour into the center of the flour and mix vigorously with a wooden spoon until glossy.

7. When the mixture is cool enough to handle, use hands and knead it into a ball.

8. Divide the mixture into two-thirds and one-third, placing the one-thirds portion in an oiled plastic bag to prevent drying out.

9. Use the two-thirds portion to line the base and sides of a 7 inch spring-form pan, pressing it down and moulding it into position.

10. Spoon in the mushroom filling, press down firmly making a "dome" shape.

11. Roll out the remaining dough to just larger than the pan and place on top of the pie, pinching the edges together to seal.

12. Trim off excess dough and glaze generously with beaten egg.

13. Cut or prick vents in the lid to allow the steam to escape.

14. Bake at 425°F for 20 minutes. Reduce to 375°F and bake for a further hour.

15. Unmold and serve on an attractive platter garnished with parsley and slices of lemon and cucumber.

TIME: Preparation takes about 35 minutes,
    cooking takes 1 hour 20 minutes.

NUTTY SPAGHETTI

An easy-to-make lunch or supper dish.

SERVES 4

8 oz spaghetti
3½ cups boiling, salted water
1 onion, finely chopped
2 tbsps sunflower oil
2½ tsps curry powder
¾ cup tomato juice
3 tbsps crunchy peanut butter
1 tbsp lemon juice
Lemon slices and peanuts for garnish

1. Boil the spaghetti until just tender and drain well.

2. Heat oil in a saucepan and fry the onion until golden brown.

3. Stir in the curry powder, tomato juice, peanut butter and lemon juice.

4. Simmer for 5 minutes and then stir into the spaghetti.

TIME: Preparation takes about 10 minutes, cooking takes 25 minutes.

SERVING IDEA: Serve garnished with lemon twists and peanuts.

VARIATION: Almond butter and blanched almonds can be used in place of the peanut butter and peanuts.

RATATOUILLE LASAGNE

Serve with rolls and a green salad
for the perfect lunch or supper.

SERVES 4-6

6 strips spinach lasagne verdi or
   whole-wheat lasagne
2-3 tbsps olive oil
2 onions, finely chopped
2 cloves garlic, crushed
1 large eggplant, chopped
1 zucchini, sliced thinly
1 green pepper, chopped
1 red pepper, chopped
14 oz can tomatoes, chopped
2-3 tbsps tomato paste
A little vegetable stock
Salt and freshly ground black pepper

White sauce
2 tbsps butter or margarine
2 tbsps whole-wheat flour
1¼ cups milk

⅓ cup Parmesan cheese, grated
Fresh parsley, to garnish

1. Preheat the oven to 350°F.

2. Cook the lasagne in boiling, salted water for 12-15 minutes.

3. Plunge pasta into a bowl of cold water to prevent overcooking or sticking.

4. Heat the oil in a large saucepan and fry the onion and garlic until soft.

5. Add the eggplant, zucchini and peppers and sauté until soft.

6. Add the tomatoes with their juice and the tomato paste and simmer until tender. It may be necessary to add a little stock at this stage.

7. Season well and set aside.

8. Make the white sauce by melting the butter in a small saucepan.

9. Add the flour and cook to a roux.

10. Add the milk slowly, stirring constantly, bring to the boil and simmer for about 5 minutes. Remove from the heat.

11. Grease a deep ovenproof dish.

12. Layer the ratatouille and lasagne strips, starting with the ratatouille and finishing with a layer of lasagne.

13. Pour over the white sauce and sprinkle the Parmesan cheese over the top.

14. Bake in the oven for 35 minutes until golden. Garnish with parsley before serving.

TIME: Preparation takes about 20 minutes, cooking takes 1 hour.

VARIATION: Three cups sliced mushrooms can be used instead of the eggplant.

ZUCCHINI AND CARROT LAYER

Serve with a sprouted salad for a light lunch or
sprinkled with fresh herbs for a special occasion.

SERVES 4

7-8 carrots, cooked, mashed and
   seasoned
1 tbsp oil
1 medium onion
3 cups zucchini, finely chopped
1 cup almonds, finely chopped or
   ground
¾ cup whole-wheat breadcrumbs
1 tsp vegetable bouillon dissolved in
   a little boiling water
1 egg, beaten
½ tsp dried, mixed herbs
1 tbsp tomato paste
1 tbsps shoyu sauce (Japanese soy sauce)
Freshly ground black pepper

1. Grease and line a 7½ x 4 inch loaf pan.

2. Heat the oil in a large saucepan and fry the onion and zucchini; remove from the heat and add all the remaining ingredients except the carrot, and mix together well.

3. Place half of the zucchini mixture into the loaf pan and press down well.

4. Arrange the carrots on top of this followed by the remaining zucchini mixture.

5. Cover with foil and bake for 1 hour at 350°F.

6. Allow to cool for 10 minutes before removing from pan.

TIME: Preparation, including cooking the carrots, takes 25 minutes.

COOK'S TIP: This mixture makes a delicious filling for a pie.

VEGETABLE CRISP

*A variety of hearty vegetables topped with oats and
cheese makes the perfect winter meal.*

SERVES 4-6

Topping
⅓ cup butter or margarine
1 cup whole-wheat flour
½ cup oatmeal
1 cup cheddar cheese, grated
¼ tsp salt

¾ cup vegetable stock or water
1¼ cups apple cider
1 tsp brown sugar
2 carrots, chopped
2 large parsnips, cut into rings
2 celery stalks, chopped
2 heads broccoli, cut into florets
¼ cauliflower, cut into florets
2 tsps whole-wheat flour
2 tbsps fresh parsley, chopped
1 medium onion, chopped and fried until
  golden
4 large tomatoes, peeled and sliced
1 cup cooked black-eyed peas
Salt and pepper

1. Make the topping by rubbing the butter into the flour and oats until the mixture resembles breadcrumbs.

2. Stir in the cheese and salt.

3. Mix the stock with the cider and sugar and put into a large pan with the carrots and parsnips.

4. Cook until just tender, remove the vegetables and put aside.

5. Add the celery, broccoli and cauliflower to the pan, cook until tender, remove and reserve with other vegetables.

6. Mix the flour with a little water, add to the cider and cook until thickened, stirring all the time.

7. Cook for 2-3 minutes, remove from the heat and add the parsley.

8. Place the onions, vegetables, tomatoes and beans in a greased casserole dish and season well. Pour the sauce over the mixture.

9. Sprinkle the topping over the top and press down a little.

10. Bake at 400°F for 30-35 minutes or until the topping is golden brown.

TIME: Preparation takes 20 minutes, cooking takes 1 hour 5 minutes.

SERVING IDEA: Serve with roast potatoes.

COOK'S TIP: The casserole can be prepared in advance to the end of Step 9.
Refrigerate until ready to cook.

SAVORY BEAN POT

Serve this exciting mixture with rice or baked potatoes and a salad.

SERVES 4

2 tbsps vegetable oil
2 vegetable bouillon cubes, crumbled
2 medium onions, chopped
2 apples, peeled and grated
2 medium carrots, grated
3 tbsps tomato paste
1¼ cups water
2 tbsps white wine vinegar
1 tbsp dried mustard
1 tsp oregano
1 tsp cumin
2 tsps brown sugar
Salt and pepper
3 cups cooked red kidney beans
A little sour cream

1. Heat the oil in a non-stick pan.

2. Add the crumbled bouillon cubes, onions, apples and carrots.

3. Sauté for 5 minutes, stirring continuously.

4. Mix the tomato paste with the water and add together with all the other ingredients except the beans and cream.

5. Stir well, cover and simmer for 2 minutes.

6. Add the beans and transfer the mixture into an ovenproof casserole.

7. Cover and bake at 350°F for 35-40 minutes.

8. Add a little more water after 20 minutes if necessary.

9. Top with swirls of sour cream and serve.

TIME: Preparation takes 20 minutes, cooking takes 45 minutes.

VARIATION: Use cider vinegar in place of the white wine vinegar.

Tomato and Pepper Quiche

Make quiche a more filling meal with a selection of salads.

SERVES 4

Pie Crust
1 cup whole-wheat flour
Pinch of salt
¼ cup vegetable fat
A little cold water to mix

Filling
2 tbsps butter or margarine
1 onion, finely chopped
½ green pepper, finely sliced
½ red pepper, finely sliced
2 tomatoes, finely sliced
3 eggs
1¼ cups heavy cream
Salt and pepper
2 tbsps Parmesan cheese

1. Mix the flour and salt together.

2. Cut the fat into small pieces and rub into the flour until the mixture resembles fine breadcrumbs.

3. Add the water and mix until a ball of dough is formed.

4. Roll out to line a 8 inch pie or quiche dish.

5. Prick the bottom lightly with a fork and bake at 350°F for 15 minutes.

6. Remove from the oven.

7. Meanwhile, melt the butter or margarine in a frying pan and sauté the onion and pepper until just softened.

8. Arrange the onion and pepper on the bottom of the crust followed by the sliced tomatoes.

9. Beat the eggs, and add the cream and seasoning.

10. Pour over the vegetables and sprinkle the cheese on top.

11. Return to the oven for 35-40 minutes until risen and golden brown on top.

TIME: Preparation takes 25 minutes, cooking takes 55 minutes.

VARIATION: For an everyday quiche, replace the cream with milk.

VEGETABLE STEW WITH HERB DUMPLINGS

The ideal meal to warm up a cold winter's night.

SERVE 4-6

1 large onion
5 cups mixed vegetables (carrot, rutabaga,
    parsnips, turnips, cauliflower etc.)
2½ cups vegetable stock
Salt and pepper
Flour to thicken

Dumplings
1 cup whole-wheat flour
2 tsps baking powder
¼ cup vegetable shortening
½ tsp dried mixed herbs
¼ tsp salt

1. Chop the onion into large pieces.

2. Peel and prepare the vegetables and chop into bite-sized pieces.

3. Put the onion and vegetables into a pan and cover with the stock.

4. Bring to the boil and simmer for 20 minutes.

5. Season to taste.

6. Mix 1 tbsp flour with a little water and stir into the stew to thicken. Add more, if needed.

7. Place the ingredients for the dumplings into a bowl and rub together until they resemble breadcrumbs. Add just enough water to bind.

8. Shape the mixture into 8 small dumplings.

9. Bring the stew to the boil and drop in the dumplings.

10. Cover and allow to simmer for 10 minutes or until dumplings are light and tender.

11. Serve at once.

TIME: Preparation takes 10 minutes, cooking takes 30 minutes.

SERVING IDEA: Serve with boiled potatoes.

VARIATION: The mixed herbs may be omitted when making the dumplings or chopped fresh parsley and a squeeze of lemon juice may be used instead.

SAVORY RICE CAKE

An excellent way to use up leftover rice.

SERVES 2-4

1 medium onion, finely chopped
1 clove garlic, crushed
2 tbsps olive oil
1 tbsp fresh thyme, chopped or ½ tbsp
    dried thyme
1 red pepper, thinly sliced
1 green pepper, thinly sliced
4 eggs, beaten
Salt and pepper
6 tbsps cooked brown rice
3 tbsps plain yogurt
¾ cup cheddar cheese, grated

1. Heat oil in an ovenproof pan and fry the onion and garlic until soft.

2. Add the thyme and peppers and fry gently for 4-5 minutes.

3. Beat the eggs with the salt and pepper.

4. Add the cooked rice to the pan followed by the eggs.

5. Cook over a moderate heat for a few minutes, stirring occasionally until the eggs are cooked underneath.

6. Spoon the yogurt on top of the part-set egg and sprinkle the cheese over the top.

7. Put under the broiler about 4 inches from the heat and cook until puffed and golden.

8. Serve immediately.

TIME: Preparation takes about 15 minutes, cooking takes 15 minutes.

SERVING IDEA: Garnish with fresh thyme or parsley and serve with a green salad.

Zucchini Mediterranean Style

*Zucchini originally came from Italy, so why
not give them the continental treatment!*

SERVES 4

3 tbsps olive oil
1 large onion, finely chopped
3 cloves garlic, crushed
1 red pepper, chopped
1 cup cooked navy beans
14 oz tomatoes
3 cups zucchini, finely sliced
½ tsp dried oregano
Salt and pepper

1. Heat the oil in a pan.

2. Add the onion, garlic and pepper and cook for 4-5 minutes.

3. Add the cooked beans, canned tomatoes and zucchini. Stir well.

4. Add the oregano and seasoning, and stir again.

5. Cover and cook slowly for 30 minutes.

TIME: Preparation takes 10-15 minutes, cooking takes 40 minutes.

SERVING IDEA: Serve on a bed of white rice.

COOK'S TIP: This dish will reheat well.

LENTIL MOUSSAKA

Try a taste of the Greek Islands with this classic dish.

SERVES 4-6

1¼ cups green lentils
1 large eggplant, sliced
4-5 tbsps oil
1 large onion, chopped
1 clove garlic, crushed
1 large carrot, diced
4 celery stalks, finely chopped
½-1 tsp dried mixed herbs
14 oz can tomatoes
2 tsps shoyu sauce (Japanese soy sauce)
Black pepper
2 medium potatoes, cooked and sliced
2 large tomatoes, sliced

Sauce
4 tbsps margarine
4 tbsps brown rice flour
Scant 2 cups milk
1 large egg, separated
½ cup grated cheddar cheese
1 tsp nutmeg

1. Cook the lentils in plenty of water until soft. Drain and reserve the liquid.

2. Fry the eggplant in the oil, drain well, leaving some of the oil in the pan, and set the eggplant aside.

3. Sauté the onion, garlic, carrot, and celery in the remaining oil and then add a little of the lentil stock.

4. Simmer with the lid on until just tender.

5. Add the lentils, mixed herbs and canned tomatoes. Simmer gently for 3-4 minutes. .

6. Season with the shoyu sauce and pepper.

7. Place a layer of the lentil mixture in a casserole dish and cover with half of the eggplant slices.

8. Cover the eggplant slices with half of the potato slices and all the tomato.

9. Repeat with the remaining lentils, eggplant and potatoes.

10. To make the sauce, melt the margarine in a saucepan, remove from the heat and stir in the flour to make a roux.

11. Add the milk gradually, blending well, so that the sauce is smooth and lump free.

12. Return to the heat and stir continually until the sauce thickens.

13. Remove the pan from the heat and cool slightly. Add the egg yolk, stir in the cheese and add the nutmeg.

14. Beat the egg white until it is stiff, then carefully fold into the sauce.

15. Pour the sauce over the moussaka, covering the dish completely.

16. Bake at 350°F for about 40 minutes until the top is golden brown and puffy.

TIME: Preparation takes 45 minutes, cooking takes 1 hour 10 minutes.

FREEZING: Assemble the mixture without the sauce and freeze. Defrost, add the sauce and cook from Step 14.

SERVING IDEA: Serve with a crunchy green salad and bread.

VEGETARIAN PAELLA

Perfect served with crusty bread and a green salad.

SERVES 4-6

4 tbsps olive oil
1 large onion, chopped
2 cloves garlic, crushed
½ tsp paprika
1½ cups long grain brown rice
3¾ cups vegetable stock
¾ cups dry white wine
14 oz can tomatoes, plus juice, chopped
1 tbsp tomato paste
½ tsp tarragon
½ tsp dried basil
½ tsp dried oregano
1 red pepper, coarsely chopped
1 green pepper, coarsely chopped
3 celery stalks, finely chopped
3 cups mushrooms, washed and sliced
½ cup snow peas, topped and tailed and
  cut into halves
⅔ cup frozen peas
½ cup cashew nuts, chopped
Salt and pepper
Fresh parsley, chopped
Lemon wedges and olives to garnish

1. Heat the oil and fry the onion and garlic until soft.

2. Add the paprika and rice and continue to cook for 4-5 minutes until the rice is transparent. Stir occasionally.

3. Add the stock, wine, tomatoes, tomato paste and herbs and simmer for 10-15 minutes.

4. Add the peppers, celery, mushrooms and snow peas and continue to cook for another 30 minutes until the rice is cooked.

5. Add the peas, cashew nuts and seasoning to taste.

6. Heat through and place on a large heated serving dish.

7. Sprinkle the parsley over the top and garnish with lemon wedges and olives.

TIME: Preparation takes 20 minutes, cooking takes 45 minutes.

COOK'S TIP: To prepare in advance, undercook slightly, add a little more stock or water and reheat. Do not add the peas until just before serving to prevent them losing their color.

ASPARAGUS AND OLIVE QUICHE

An interesting combination which gives
a new twist to a classic dish.

MAKES 2 QUICHES

2 10 inch part baked pie crusts (see recipe for Corn and Parsnip Quiche)
6 eggs
2½ cups heavy cream
1 tsp salt
Pinch of nutmeg
Salt and pepper
2 tbsps flour
2 cans green asparagus tips
¾ cup green olives
2 onions, finely chopped and sautéed in a little butter until soft
¾ cup cheddar cheese, grated
2 tbsps Parmesan cheese
4 tbsps butter

1. Whisk the eggs with the cream.

2. Add the salt, nutmeg and seasoning.

3. Add a little of the cream mixture to the flour and mix until smooth, then add to the cream mixture.

4. Arrange the asparagus tips, olives and onions in the pie crusts and pour the cream mixture over the top.

5. Sprinkle with the grated cheddar and Parmesan cheese.

6. Dot with the butter and bake at 375°F for 25 minutes.

7. Turn down the oven to 350°F and bake for another further 15 minutes until the quiches are golden.

TIME: Preparation takes 20 minutes, cooking takes 40 minutes.

FREEZING: The quiches may be frozen but a slightly better result is obtained if you freeze the pie crusts and add the filling just before baking.

SAVORY GRAIN CASSEROLE

Serve as a complete meal for 2 people or serve
accompanied with lightly steamed vegetables for 4 people.

SERVES 2-4

½ cup brown rice
½ cup split peas
2 celery stalks, very finely chopped
1 medium onion, very finely chopped
1½ cups mushrooms, chopped
14 oz canned tomatoes, drained and
　　chopped or 5 tomatoes, peeled and
　　chopped
½ tsp dill seeds
¼ tsp dried thyme
2 tbsps shoyu sauce (Japanese soy sauce)
1 egg, beaten
1 cup cheddar cheese, grated

1. Cover the rice with water and cook for 10-15 minutes; drain.

2. Cover the split peas with water and cook for 20 minutes until just tender but not mushy; drain.

3. Meanwhile, combine the celery, onion, mushrooms, tomatoes, dill, thyme, shoyu sauce and the egg in a large bowl.

4. Stir in the rice and peas.

5. Place the mixture in a greased ovenproof casserole and cook for 45 minutes at 350°F.

6. Remove from the oven and sprinkle with the grated cheese.

7. Return to the oven for 10 minutes until the cheese has melted.

8. Serve at once.

TIME: Preparation takes 10 minutes, cooking takes 1 hour 45 minutes.

SERVING IDEA: Garnish with a few whole cooked mushrooms or broiled tomatoes.

Vegetarian Shepherd's Pie

This pie will serve 2 people without any
accompaniments and 4 people if served with vegetables.

SERVES 2-4

Scant 2 cups vegetable stock or water
1 tsp yeast extract
½ cup brown lentils
¼ cup pearl barley
1 large carrot, diced
½ onion, chopped finely
1 clove garlic, crushed
½ cup walnuts, coarsely chopped
1 tsp vegetarian gravy powder or flour
Salt and pepper
3 medium potatoes, cooked and mashed

1. Heat 1¼ cups of the stock with the yeast extract, add the lentils and barley and simmer for 30 minutes.

2. Heat remaining stock in a saucepan and cook the carrot, onion, garlic and walnuts for 15 minutes until tender.

3. Mix the gravy powder or flour with a little water and add to the carrot mixture; stir over a low heat until thickened.

4. Combine the lentils and barley with the carrot mixture, season and place in an ovenproof dish.

5. Cover with the mashed potato and bake at 350°F for about 30 minutes until browned on top.

TIME: Preparation takes 15 minutes, cooking takes 1 hour.

SERVING IDEA: Garnish with broiled tomatoes and serve with vegetables in season, broccoli, sprouts, cabbage etc.

BUTTER BEAN ONE-POT

This is a quick to make, all-in-one dish.

SERVES 4

2 tbsps vegetable oil
1 green pepper, finely chopped
1 large onion, finely chopped
2 celery stalks, diced
14 oz can tomatoes
2 large potatoes, peeled and diced
1¼ cups vegetable stock or water
2 tbsps finely chopped parsley
Salt and pepper
2 cups cooked butter beans or lima beans

1. Heat the oil in a large saucepan and add the pepper, onion and celery, and cook gently until the onion begins to brown.

2. Add the tomatoes and their juice, the potatoes, stock, parsley, salt and pepper.

3. Simmer for about 30 minutes or until the liquid is reduced by half.

4. Add the beans and heat through gently for 5-10 minutes.

TIME: Preparation takes about 15 minutes, cooking takes 50 minutes.

SERVING IDEA: Serve with lots of crusty bread. Garlic bread also goes well with this dish.

TOFU BURGERS

*Serve these delicious burgers with mustard and
chutney and accompany with a salad.*

MAKES 8

½ cup bulgar wheat
½ cup boiling water
1 small onion, very finely chopped
1 small carrot, grated
¾ cup mushrooms, very finely chopped
9 oz package tofu
¼ tsp dried basil
¼ tsp dried oregano
2 tbsps shoyu sauce (Japanese soy sauce)
1 tsp tomato paste
Freshly ground black pepper
Whole-wheat flour
Oil for deep frying

1. Put the bulgar wheat into a bowl and cover with boiling water. Leave for 15 minutes until all the water has been absorbed.

2. Add the onion, carrot and mushrooms to the bulgar and mix well.

3. Drain the tofu and crumble into the bulgar mixture.

4. Add the basil, oregano, shoyu, tomato paste, a little black pepper and 1 tablespoon of whole-wheat flour. Mix together well.

5. With wet hands, take heaped tablespoonfuls of the mixture, squeeze together well and shape into burgers.

6. Coat the burgers with whole-wheat flour.

7. Heat the oil until very hot and fry the burgers 3 or 4 at a time until golden brown.

8. Remove and drain on paper towels.

TIME: Preparation takes 15 minutes, cooking takes 5 minutes per batch.

WATCHPOINT: The oil must be very hot otherwise the burgers will disintegrate.

FREEZING: It is well worthwhile doubling the quantity and freezing a batch of burgers. Freeze for up to 3 months. Reheat by broiling or warming in the oven.

CAROB APPLE CAKE

This cake is nicer if kept in an airtight container for a day before serving.

MAKES 1 CAKE

⅔ cup soft margarine
½ cup light brown sugar
1 large egg, beaten
1½ cups fine whole-wheat flour
5 tbsps carob powder
1½ tsps baking powder
1 tbsp Amontillado sherry (medium dry)
2¾ cups apples, peeled and sliced

Topping
½ cup carob chips
1 tbsp butter
A little water

1. Cream the margarine and sugar together until fluffy.

2. Add half of the beaten egg and continue creaming.

3. Add the rest of the egg together with the flour, carob and baking powder and sherry.

4. Spoon half of the mixture into a round 8 inch cake pan and cover with the sliced apples.

5. Add the other half of the mixture and smooth the top.

6. Bake at 325°F for 1¼ hours or until firm to the touch.

7. Melt the carob chips with the butter and water and drizzle over the top of the cake.

TIME: Preparation takes 25 minutes, cooking takes 1¼ hours.

SERVING IDEA: Serve hot with yogurt or cold with tea or coffee.

WINDWARD FRUIT BASKET

An impressive dessert that is surprisingly easy to prepare.

SERVES 4-6

1 large ripe melon (see Cook's Tip)
2 apples
Juice of 1 lime
2 mangoes
2 kiwi fruit
2 cups strawberries
1 cup raspberries
3 tbsps honey
2 tbsps dark rum
4 tbsps butter

1. Cut the top off the melon and scoop out the seeds.

2. Using a melon baller, scoop out balls of melon and place in a large bowl.

3. Remove the core from the apples, dice and toss in the lime juice.

4. Peel and chop the mangoes.

5. Peel and slice the kiwi fruit.

6. Combine all the fruits.

7. Heat the honey, rum and butter gently until the butter has melted.

8. Cool, and pour over the fruits.

9. Toss gently and fill the melon shell with the fruit mixture.

10. Place on a serving dish and serve immediately.

TIME: Preparation takes 20 minutes, cooking takes 2 minutes.

SERVING IDEA: For a special occasion, make holes around the top of the melon with a skewer and decorate with fresh flowers.

VARIATION: Use any fresh fruits in season, pears, peaches etc.

COOK'S TIP: Use your favorite type of melon or what is available in the stores at the time.

CRANBERRY AND APPLE CRISP

Serve hot with plain yogurt or serve cold with ice cream.

SERVES 4

1½ lbs cooking apples
¼ cup sugar
1½ cups fresh cranberries
2 tbsps water

Crumble
⅓ cup butter or margarine
½ cup sunflower seeds
⅓ cup light brown sugar
1¼ cups whole-wheat flour
1 cup oatmeal

1. Peel, core and dice the apples. They should measure about 4¾ cups.

2. Cook in a saucepan with the sugar and about 2 tbsps water until slightly softened.

3. Add the cranberries and cook for a further minute. Remove from the heat.

4. Melt butter or margarine in a small saucepan and add the sunflower seeds. Fry gently for a few minutes.

5. Meanwhile, mix together the other ingredients in a large bowl, rubbing in the sugar if lumpy.

6. Pour in the butter and sunflower seeds and combine to form a loose mixture.

7. Place the fruit in a large, shallow oven-proof dish and sprinkle over the crisp topping.

8. Bake at 350°F for about 40 minutes or until the top is golden and crisp.

TIME: Preparation takes about 20 minutes, cooking takes 50 minutes.

DELUXE BREAD AND BUTTER PUDDING

Serve just as it is, hot from the oven.

SERVES 2-4

4 thin slices whole-wheat bread
A little butter
Raspberry preserve
2 eggs, beaten
Scant 2 cups milk, warmed
2 tbsps heavy cream
3 tbsps light brown sugar
1 tsp vanilla extract
2 tbsps raisins, soaked for 1 hour
1 tbsp dates
Grated nutmeg

1. Remove the crusts from the bread.

2. Sandwich the bread with the butter and preserve and cut into small triangles.

3. Beat the eggs until fluffy.

4. Add the warmed milk, cream, sugar and vanilla.

5. Stir together well, making sure that the sugar has dissolved.

6. Arrange the bread triangles in a lightly buttered ovenproof dish so that they overlap and stand up slightly.

7. Scatter the dried fruits over the top.

8. Pour the egg, cream and milk mixture into the dish, ensuring that the bread triangles are saturated.

9. Grate a little nutmeg over the pudding and bake at 400°F for about 30 minutes.

TIME: Preparation takes 10 minutes, cooking takes 30 minutes.

VARIATION: Other flavored preserves may be used instead of raspberry preserve.

Index

Photography by Peter Barry
Recipes styled by Helen Burdett
Designed by Richard Hawke

The publishers are indebted to Chris Hardisty, Freda Hooker, D.M. Arnot, Isabel A. Booth, Ian Jones, Marianne Vaney, Pam Knutson, Val Shaw, Susan Mills, Wendy Godden, Vivien Margison, Kate Allen and Sue Bliss.